300
Incredible Things
for Women
on the
Internet

300INCREDIBLE.COM, LLC
600 Village Trace, Building 23
Marietta, Georgia 30067

(800) 909-6505

ISBN 1-930435-05-3

— Dedication —

To those women of all ages who are dedicated to making this a better world. May the Internet inspire you and help nurture your love of learning.

Introduction

The Internet can be an incredibly useful tool for saving time and money, and for making your everyday life easier. However, there is much interference and noise on the Net. We have filtered out all the clutter, so you can enjoy the Internet for its intended purposes. Whatever your interests are, we have included something for everyone. So, kick off your shoes, sit back, relax and enjoy the journey.

Robyn Spizman
http://www.robynspizman.com

Ken Leebow
Leebow@300INCREDIBLE.COM
http://www.300INCREDIBLE.com

About the Authors

Robyn Spizman is a consumer advocate with more than seventeen years of experience as "The Super Shopper" and "Super Mom" on network television. Nationally known for her consumer advice, Robyn's lively, high-energy segments have been featured extensively in media appearances on *CNN*, *The Discovery Channel*, *CNBC*, *CNNFN*, *Roseanne*, *Good Day New York*, *ABC Radio Network*, and *National Public Radio*. A former educator, she has authored over sixty books, including award-winning titles in the fields of education, parenting and self help.

Robyn lives in Atlanta with her husband and two children, who get all the credit for helping Mom get online and become a Web wiz.

Ken Leebow has been involved with the computer business for over twenty years. The Internet has fascinated him since he began exploring it several years ago, and he has helped over a million readers utilize its resources. Ken has appeared frequently in the media, educating individuals about the Web's greatest hits. He is considered a leading expert on what is incredible about the Internet.

When not online, you can find Ken playing tennis, running, reading or spending time with his family. He is living proof that being addicted to the Net doesn't mean giving up on the other pleasures of life.

Acknowledgments

Putting a book together requires many expressions of appreciation. The following people deserve our special thanks:

- Robyn's family—Willy, Justin and Ali—for providing steady sources of inspiration and happiness.

- Suzi Brozman, for providing especially helpful research assistance.

- Ken's family—Denice, Alissa and Josh—for being especially supportive during the writing of the book.

- Paul Joffe and Janet Bolton, of *TBI Creative Services*, for their editing and graphics skills.

- Mark Krasner and Janice Caselli for sharing the vision of the book and helping make it a reality.

The Incredible Internet Book Series

300 Incredible Things to Do on the Internet

300 More Incredible Things to Do on the Internet

300 Incredible Things for Kids on the Internet

300 Incredible Things for Sports Fans on the Internet

300 Incredible Things for Golfers on the Internet

300 Incredible Things for Travelers on the Internet

300 Incredible Things for Health, Fitness & Diet on the Internet

300 Incredible Things for Auto Racing Fans on the Internet

300 Incredible Things for Self-Help & Wellness on the Internet

300 Incredible Things to Learn on the Internet

300 Incredible Things for Home Improvement on the Internet

300 Incredible Things for Seniors on the Internet

300 Incredible Things for Pet Lovers on the Internet

300 Incredible Things for Women on the Internet

America Online Web Site Directory
Where to Go for What You Need

TABLE OF CONTENTS

TABLE OF CONTENTS (continued)

CHAPTER I
SIMPLY THE BEST

1
It Takes a Village

http://www.ivillage.com
Perhaps the ultimate women's site, this is a global village for every aspect of your life, from "astrology" to "work," with stops at finance, health, beauty, politics and more.

2
I am Woman

http://www.women.com
This is a celebration of women's hopes, desires, concerns and questions, divided into easy-to-access channels.

3
A Breath of Fresh Air

http://www.oxygen.com
It's online, it's on-air, and it's for women, by women. Oxygen reflects your life and the issues that concern you. You'll also have the chance to tell your story via chats and message boards.

4
Home is Where the Heart Is

http://www.homearts.com
In addition to sections for home, health, family, money and food, you'll find links to many popular women's magazines.

5
Join the Forum

http://www.womensforum.com
This grassroots portal has been developed to profile women's sites, leading you to over a hundred sites of interest.

6
Women's World

http://www.wwwomen.com
Here's everything from politics to sports, health and humor, home and family, with links galore to just about any topic you could want to explore and a search engine to help you find it all.

7
It's a Woman Thing
http://www.herplanet.com
This planet is all about women, and it's made up of many Web sites that address issues for home life, business and the Internet. You'll even find a section on "Women to Watch."

8
Hip Click
http://www.chickclick.com
This cool site is dedicated to women of "Generation I" (Internet).

9
Let's Make a Plan
http://www.womenplanning.com
The mission is "to disseminate information and educational materials on all aspects of pre-retirement planning, and to help women of all ages achieve financial security."

10
Your Guide
http://www.womerica.com
From beauty to weddings, this Internet portal designed specifically for women will lead you to many interesting Web sites.

11
The World at Your Command
http://www.sheknows.com
http://www.pleiades-net.com
Click on sites such as health, career, family and much more, from lipstick to law school, chat to careers, consumer guides to city guides.

12
Listen to the Music
http://www.womenonair.com
This radio show takes the listener on a trip around the world, through the multicultural genres of the most talented female artists working yesterday, today and tomorrow.

13
A Place Where…
http://www.clubmom.com
…you'll be recognized, rewarded and respected for doing one of the hardest, most important jobs there is!

14
Embrace It
http://www.embracingmotherhood.com
The philosophy of this site is: "In order to take care of others, you must first learn to take care of yourself." Embrace this site and take a free six-week course, read the many quotes and learn from its tips.

15
A Girl Thing
http://www.beinggirl.com
Brought to you by the manufacturers of Tampax, this site addresses many of the issues that teens face.

16
<u>A Girlfriend is…</u>

http://www.girlfriendsguide.com

…someone who forgives you when you forget her birthday. She is someone who has heard your favorite stories a million times, but still acts interested whenever you repeat them.

17
<u>Total Woman</u>

http://www.totalwoman.com

"Our content focuses on the themes that are at the core of every woman's life: our health, our work, our relationships with friends, husbands, lovers and children, and our curiosity about the world around us."

18
<u>Independent Women's Forum</u>

http://www.iwf.org

The mission of the Independent Women's Forum is to affirm women's participation in and contributions to a free, self-governing society.

19
Can We Chat?

http://www.women2women.com
Here's what they say: "We hope you'll relax and make yourself at home here. Our goal is a community which provides support, resources, fun and education for adult women about their life choices."

20
TV Women Love

http://www.oprah.com
http://www.rosie.com
Oprah and Rosie address your interests, loves, concerns and deepest worries. They are smart, sassy, funny, serious, spiritual and—most of all—inspirational.

21
Lifetime TV

http://www.lifetimetv.com
The online version of this cable television network addresses health, career, money, relationships, home life and much more.

22
It's a Good Thing

http://www.marthastewart.com
Online, enjoy Martha Stewart twenty-four hours a day.

23
Read All About It!

http://www.msmagazine.com
http://www.lhj.com
http://www.mccalls.com
http://www.womansday.com

These online magazines are devoted to your needs, with articles and departments addressing every facet of today's woman.

24
Women's Financial Network

http://www.wfn.com
This network is designed to provide women access to the information and tools they need to better understand and manage their finances.

25
Women in Business

http://www.womanowned.com
http://www.dol.gov/dol/wb
http://www.bizwomen.com
These sites offer products and services for small business owners. They also provide networking opportunities and resources for women who are starting or growing their own companies.

26
You Count

http://www.count-me-in.org
Count Me In is an organization that makes small business loans and gives training scholarships to women.

27
Digital Women

http://www.digital-women.com
This site is for businesswomen to gather tips and to network with each other.

28
Women in Computing
http://www.girlgeeks.com
If you're involved in computing and the high-tech world, this hip and colorful site is better than hanging out at the water cooler.

29
It's Only a Game
http://www.discoverbusiness.com
Receive $100,000 (in play money) and operate your own business.

30
My Career
http://www.careerbabe.com
http://www.monster.com
http://www.headhunter.com
http://www.vault.com
These are some of the biggest job search engines, with tips, career resources, resume help, online job fairs and insider research.

31
Working at Home

http://www.home2work.com
http://www.hbwm.com
http://www.wahm.com
Telecommuting is the next great labor wave. Learn the basics of working from home.

32
I'm Busy

http://www.ceoexpress.com
Patricia Pomerleau says, "As a senior executive, I found my peers to be busy people with little time or patience for the Internet. The sheer volume of information and extensive time it can take to locate useful sites can be a significant deterrent for executives interested in using the Web." Here's the solution.

33
Technological Lifestyle

http://www.technocopia.com
We're now living a technology-immersed lifestyle. This site will make things easier for home, work, play and our future.

34
Women in the Arts

http://www.nmwa.org
The National Museum of Women in the Arts recognizes the achievements of women artists of all periods and nationalities by exhibiting, preserving, acquiring, and researching art by women and by educating the public about their accomplishments.

35
Women in History

http://www.greatwomen.org
http://www.nwhp.org
http://www.firstladies.org
Discover amazing stories of women of valor and achievement throughout history.

36
Famous Speeches

http://gos.sbc.edu
Gifts of Speech is dedicated to preserving and creating access to speeches made by influential contemporary women.

37
Women Involved

http://www.aauw.org
http://www.now.org
http://www.lwv.org

Check out these organizations where women can express concerns about voting, rights, education and public affairs. Your involvement can make a difference.

38
Women in Sports

http://www.womensmultisport.com
http://www.sportsforwomen.com

These online publications will keep you up to date on women's sports and fitness.

39
Sports Talk

http://www.girlstalksports.com

The goal here is "to provide one source for women to find all the sports news they want. No longer do you have to search the back pages and bottom of the fishing report for your favorite women's sport."

40
Be a Pupuliac

http://www.pupulesports.com

Its mission: "To provide an authentic sports network that will bring women's sports to the forefront, and will also encourage and support the participation of girls and women in sports and fitness activities."

41
Care Guide

http://www.careguide.com

Here's a resource guide for taking care of the elderly and the children in your life.

CHAPTER II
JUST MY STYLE

42
Aromatherapy

http://www.aromaweb.com
http://www.aromaessentials.com
Soothe thyself by learning about oils, herbs and essences. Sit back, relax and enjoy.

43
The World of Beauty

http://www.beauty.com
Beauty is the mission, and they want to help you enjoy your experience by finding the right products and having fun in the process.

44
Pretty Woman

http://www.eve.com
http://www.beautycare.com
Here are beauty secrets, tips and advice to enhance your best assets. You'll even have an opportunity to ask an expert.

"Your plastic surgery was a great success, Mrs. Jones. The lines and wrinkles are completely gone!"

45
The Secret's Out

http://www.1001beautysecrets.com
Take care of your body, mind and spirit. This site concentrates on health, beauty, nutrition and fitness.

46
Your Salon

http://www.beautynet.com
Here's your virtual salon for hair, skin, nail care and tanning. Enjoy the tips, answers to questions and chatting.

47
That Healthy Glow

http://www.pioneerthinking.com/beauty.html
http://www.healthnbeauty.com
Learn to enhance your natural beauty with natural ingredients. You can even make your own soap and lotions.

48
Meet the Cosmetic Cop

http://www.cosmeticscop.com
Paula Begoun has been educating consumers for over twenty years about cosmetics products and the industry.

49
In Style

http://www.alwaysinstyle.com
Answer a few questions, and get your personalized analysis, advice and product recommendations.

50
Get the Makeover

http://www.makeup.com
You'll find tips, advice, shopping and links to interesting makeup and fashion sites.

51
The Magazine Rack

http://www.ellemag.com
http://www.vogue.com
http://www.covergirl.com
http://www.glamour.com
http://www.cosmomag.com
http://www.seventeen.com
Read all about it — from your hair to your fingertips, there are many secrets to be discovered and fashions galore to be enjoyed.

52
About Face

http://www.clinique.com
http://www.gloss.com
http://www.avon.com
http://www.marykay.com
http://www.bobbibrowncosmetics.com
What's new in the world of makeup and fragrance? Get the answers from these beauty sources.

53
Visionary Beauty

http://www.helenarubinstein.com
Helena knows beauty on and off the Net. This Web site is worth a visit to view its beautiful design.

54
Hairs to You

http://www.hairdos.com
http://www.hairboutique.com
Your hair is your crowning glory. Keep it healthy, stylish and flattering with hints from the professionals.

55
I'll Wear That

http://www.asseenin.com
If you ever wanted to emulate your favorite celebrities, this site is for you. Find out what the people you admire wear and drive.

56
Trends in the News

http://www.fashionguide.com
http://www.fashion.net
Here's a daily look at news from the world of fashion shows, awards, designers, schools and jobs.

57
Fashion First

http://www.fashion-planet.com
http://www.firstview.com
Explore fashion news, jobs and an insider's look at designers, celebrities, the newest styles and shops.

58
Teen Fashion

http://www.fashionteen.com
Straight from Beverly Hills, this teen magazine has articles, fashion and beauty tips and a few celebrity profiles.

59
Fashion Plus

http://www.realsize.com
Fashion doesn't just come in size six. Find fashion news and shopping for generously proportioned teens and women.

60
Got Glasses

http://www.eyeglasses.com
Try them on before you buy them. Yes, even online, you can try before you buy.

CHAPTER III
WE ARE FAMILY

61
Kids' Safety Online

http://www.getnetwise.org
http://www.disney.go.com/cybersafety
Traveling the Internet safely is a concern for many families. These sites are helpful and entertaining.

62
The Stork and You

http://www.storknet.org
http://www.epregnancy.com
http://www.pregnancytoday.com
http://www.thelaboroflove.com
Learn all about your pregnancy, your body and the baby.

63
What Do I Do Now?

http://www.helioshealth.com/baby
http://www.baby-care.com
Here are terrific how-to guides that will do everything but change the diapers!

64
The Baby Everything Stores

http://www.iBaby.com
http://www.babygear.com
Coddle your bundle of joy with diapers, toys, clothes and just about everything else you can imagine.

65
What's in a Name?

http://www.babynames.com
Have some fun with possible names for your baby. Type in a name and see what it means, or type in a meaning and see what name pops up.

66
Tell the World
http://www.babiesonline.com
Create your own baby announcement Web site and show off your new addition to friends, family and the whole world.

67
Moms Network
http://www.momsnetwork.com
This site offers the tools, resources and networking that work-at-home moms need to balance the important areas of their lives.

68
Moms with Modems
http://www.cybermom.com
http://www.clubmom.com
Communicate with moms around the world. Tell your story, and listen to others from every country.

69
Moms Online

http://www.mom.com
http://www.myria.com
These are sites to support, inform and encourage mothers, with articles about kids, money, home, work, relationships, beauty, shopping and more.

70
Parent Soup

http://www.parentsoup.com
This site from iVillage.com offers a comprehensive look at parenting, from infancy to teens, with expert advice, message boards and a useful tools section.

71
Your Family and You

http://www.parentsplace.com
http://www.family.go.com
http://www.greatdayamerica.com
These are resources for the entire family, including education, parenting and hints from other parents. You'll also find all sorts of family-related articles, including sites, shopping, cooking, crafts and family relations.

72
Happy Family

http://www.happyfamilies.com
Keep it light with this humorous look at family life. There are good links to many family-related sites, funny stories, recipes and interactive avenues.

73
Mommy Times

http://www.mommytimes.com
This site is "dedicated to preserving the sanity of moms everywhere." Enjoy the monthly newsletter and parenting links galore.

74
Parental Portal

http://www.abcparenting.com
The ABC's of parenting can be found at this all-inclusive site.

"Are you trying to auction
your Brussels sprouts again?"

75
Share the Wealth

http://www.parents-talk.com
http://www.parenthoodweb.com
These parenting sites let you compare and learn from other parents' experiences.

76
Blending Families

http://www.stepfamily.net
http://www.stepfamily.org
http://www.secondwivesclub.com
These nurturing sites can help make a blended family into a successful family. Ask questions, read timely articles and share experiences with others.

77
Adoption

http://www.adopting.com
http://www.ibar.com/voices
Here are sites and resources for and about adoption.

78
Let's Talk

http://www.talkingwithkids.org
This site encourages parents to talk with kids earlier and more often about difficult but important issues.

79
Learning Central

http://www.familyeducation.com
This huge site is dedicated to your child's learning, from infancy on up.

80
Kids in the Know

http://www.yahooligans.com
http://www.webcrawler.com/ctw
http://www.connectforkids.org
http://www.surfnetkids.com
Kids are seeking answers and solutions on the Net. These kid friendly search engines are stimulating and fun.

81
<u>Surviving Your Child's Teen Years</u>

http://www.parentingteens.com
http://www.parentingadolescents.com
http://www.parenting-qa.com/teens.html
Remember, you also went through the teen years. Too bad there was no Internet to help your parents!

82
<u>Here Comes the Bride</u>

http://www.ultimatewedding.com
http://www.bridalplanner.com
http://www.theknot.com
http://www.weddingchannel.com
http://www.modernbride.com
http://www.tncweddings.com
It's your special day and you want it to be absolutely perfect. Use any of these planners to help you with every detail.

83
Grandparenting

http://www.igrandparents.com
Create a Web site to brag about the grandkids, surf to many fine sites with Grandma Betty, chat with other grandparents and much more.

84
Family Focus

http://www.myfamily.com
http://www.familypoint.com
Stay in touch the modern way. Create a Web site for sharing photos, planning events, chatting and keeping in touch.

85
Four-Legged Family Members

http://www.healthypet.com
http://www.animalnetwork.com
http://www.acmepet.com
Do a little research, and pick the right cuddly creature for your family. Then, make sure you keep it happy and healthy.

CHAPTER IV
PROTECT YOURSELF

86
Ms. Money

http://www.pinkbull.com
http://www.wife.org
http://www.msmoney.com
http://www.ka-ching.com
Fun, interesting and informative, these sites offer excellent financial guidance for today's woman.

87
Mind Your Money

http://www.familymoney.com
http://www.ivillagemoneylife.com
http://www.money.com/money/magazine/women
Here's an online guide to investing, saving, planning and using the Web, with tips, tools and a lot of advice.

88
Knowledge Brokers

http://www.cnnfn.com
http://cbs.marketwatch.com
http://www.cnbc.com
A wealth of finance-related information is just a few clicks away. These big media companies offer timely and detailed financial news and information.

89
Don't Be Foolish

http://www.fool.com
http://www.moneyminded.com
With these sites, mind your money in a fun and informative manner.

90
Take Charge

http://www.cardweb.com
http://www.bankrate.com
Plastic is big in this millennium, too. Take charge of your financial situation by being an informed consumer about credit cards.

91
Rating the Rates

http://www.rate.net
http://www.bestrate.com
Find the very best rates, fees and services for credit cards, savings accounts, certificates of deposit and loans.

92
Personal Finances

http://www.smartmoney.com
No doubt about it, this Wall Street Journal online magazine will make you smarter about money.

93
Compare Notes

http://www.investorschat.com
http://www.investingonline.org
http://www.ragingbull.com
Share your success and knowledge in these investment chat rooms. Try your hand at online investing, or just learn how others are doing it.

94
In the Know

http://www.bigtipper.com
What are the investment pros picking? This site will tell you.

95
Mutual Funds

http://www.findafund.com
http://www.fundalarm.com
http://www.fundsinteractive.com
It's an easy way to start investing, so visit these sites and learn the ins and outs of the market.

96
College Embarkation

http://www.embark.com
http://www.finaid.org
http://www.collegeboard.com
There's a lot to learn about college—which one's right for you or your kids, and how do you go about getting in and paying for it? These sites get straight A's.

97
Insurance Guide

http://www.life-line.org
http://www.insweb.com
http://www.quickquote.com
http://www.ambest.com/ratings/search.html
Insurance is one of the most important and confusing purchases you will ever make. These sites will provide quotes and assist with understanding the insurance maze.

98
Quote Me on That

http://www.quotes123.com
This is a great source for quotes on everything from auto loans to travel insurance, with some straight talk on credit cards, consumer news, business links, magazines and investments.

99
Home Sweet Home

http://www.realtor.com
http://www.domania.com
http://www.homeadvisor.com
http://www.cyberhomes.com

Here are all the basics, including figuring how much house you can afford, finding one (over a million are listed) and getting a loan.

100
Mortgage Mania

http://www.hsh.com
http://www.mortgage101.com
http://mortgage.quicken.com

These sites will help you become an informed home buyer and consumer.

101
Moving On
http://www.relocationcentral.com
http://www.virtualrelocation.com
In our mobile society, you might need these resources. You'll discover interesting tips and tools, including a salary calculator to let you know how much you'd have to earn to maintain your lifestyle elsewhere.

102
Consumer Advocates
http://www.clarkhoward.com
http://www.consumerworld.org
These consumer advocates will keep you informed about everything from autos to travel. While you're online, listen to Clark Howard's daily radio show.

103
Show Me Some Attitude
http://www.consumerama.com
Consumer issues can often be a little bland, but not here. You'll find news, advice, commentary, protest sites and much more.

104
Stretch Your Dollars

http://www.stretcher.com
In these harried times, here's your weekly source for simple living.

105
Caution: Info Highway

http://www.scambusters.com
http://www.fraud.org
Check these sites for current information on fraud, counterfeiting, fee schemes, viruses and more to beware of as you travel the Net.

106
The Educated Shopper

http://www.productreviewnet.com
http://www.consumerreview.com
Want to be an educated consumer? Stop here to get independent product reviews.

107
Recall City

http://www.childrecall.com
http://www.consumer.gov
Need to know about products that have been recalled? These sites have the word.

108
Car Knowledge

http://www.edmunds.com
http://www.kbb.com
Be in the know before you go. Approach car dealers with as much information as they have, to ensure the best deal for yourself.

109
Tips and Advice

http://www.carbuyingtips.com
http://www.ivillage.com/auto
Car dealers hate 'em, but you'll love getting valuable tips and tools from these sites.

"I went to a time management seminar last week.
I've decided to cut 'save the world' from my to-do list."

110
Car Buying Online

http://carpoint.msn.com
http://www.carsdirect.com
http://www.autoweb.com
http://www.autobytel.com
No more tire kicking. These are some of the major car buying services online.

111
To Lease or Buy?

http://www.leasesource.com
http://www.smartmoney.com/lease
Make an informed decision when leasing your next automobile. Learn the facts, and do your figuring here before negotiating a lease.

112
Deals on Wheels

http://www.alldata.com
http://www.autotown.com
Get all the data you need about auto repair and recall.

113
Auto Safety and Fuel Economy

http://www.fueleconomy.gov
http://www.crashtest.com
Is your car a gas guzzler? How well does it do in crash tests? Check it out.

114
Take My Advice

http://www.freeadvice.com
Do you understand your rights? This site provides general information for more than a hundred legal topics.

115
It's the Law!

http://www.nolo.com
http://www.uslaw.com
http://www.legaldocs.com
http://www.gigalaw.com
Here are legal resources for individuals, small businesses and employee groups, with books, forms and answers to most of your legal questions.

116
Portal to Law

http://www.findlaw.com
http://www.lawresearch.com
If it has to do with law, these research and directory sites will help you, from A to Z.

117
Divorce Court

http://www.divorcesupport.com
http://www.divorcenet.com
http://www.divorcesource.com
Over fifty percent of marriages end in divorce. If you require detailed information, advice or tips on any aspect of divorce, these sites are here to support you.

118
Need a Lawyer?

http://www.lawyers.com
http://www.lawoffice.com
The Internet has much to offer in the legal arena. If you need to find an attorney, these sites list every lawyer in the land.

CHAPTER V
GET PHYSICAL

119
Health on the Net

http://www.hon.ch
http://www.hiethics.org
These sites have principles to guide health Web sites and promote high standards. Visit here before exploring the world of health on the Net.

120
Women's Health

http://www.womens-health.com
Empower yourself with channels for assessing, learning, interacting and acting on health issues.

121
Health and Human Services

http://www.4women.org
This department provides health information and a referral center for women.

122
Topics Galore

http://www.womenfirst.com
From acupuncture to yoga, you'll find over fifty topics specific to women's health.

123
Thrive Online

http://www.thriveonline.com
This site has great information on medical issues, fitness, sexuality, nutrition and weight loss. May we all thrive, online and offline.

124
Holistic Health

http://www.herhealth.com
http://www.healthwell.com
Many of the health issues that affect women are discussed here from a holistic perspective. You'll also find current news items.

125
Intelligent Choices

http://www.webmd.com
http://www.mayohealth.org
http://www.intelihealth.com
These sites make health and medical information accessible to the widest possible audience. Most issues are addressed, and you'll find many tools to assist with your ongoing healthcare.

126
Portals to Health

http://www.achoo.com
http://www.medexplorer.com
http://www.mediconsult.com
http://www.healthfinder.gov
There are many places on the Net that will lead you to many other health sites. Let these sites be your gateways.

127
Online Pharmacy

http://www.rxlist.com
http://www.merck-medco.com
Learn about drugs and their interactions. If you need to fill a prescription, you can do that, too.

128
Alternative Medicine

http://www.earthmed.com
http://www.alternativemedicine.com
http://www.altmedicine.com
Use these centers to seek alternative medicine information and holistic healing links.

129
The Doctor Will See You Now

http://www.drkoop.com
http://www.drweil.com
http://www.drbernie.com
http://www.drruth.com

These well-known and respected doctors have established homes on the Web.
Whether it's about general healthcare, natural, disease or sex, these docs are ready,
willing and able to help.

130
Infertility

http://www.resolve.org

This non-profit organization's mission is to provide timely, compassionate support
and information to people who are experiencing infertility and to increase awareness
of infertility issues through public education and advocacy.

131
Kids Health

http://www.healthykids.com

Here's a site dedicated to raising happy and healthy children.

132
Attention Deficit Disorder

http://www.chadd.org
http://www.oneaddplace.com
http://www.adda-sr.org
These are comprehensive sites with articles, resources and support for families dealing with ADHD and other learning difficulties.

133
Cancer Awareness

http://www.nationalbreastcancer.org
http://www.thebreastclinic.com
http://www.cancerhelp.com
Being informed is half the battle. Explore—don't ignore—this major threat to women.

134
Breast Health

http://www.ibreast.com
http://www.imammagram.com
Evaluate news, research and the value of computer-aided detection.

135
Menopause

http://www.power-surge.com
Chats, newsletters, experts and more will assist you through this time of your life.

136
A Healthy Mind

http://www.mentalhelp.net
http://www.mentalhealth.org
Keep mentally fit. These mental health directories and guides are for your own peace of mind.

137
Prevention Magazine

http://www.prevention.com
A long-time staple for many, this publication has many great articles about health, fitness, weight loss and food.

138
Feelin' Good!

http://www.24hourfitness.com
http://www.fitnessonline.com
Tips, experts, calculators, a personal profile and answers to your questions on fitness, nutrition, exercise and health can all be found at these sites.

139
Fitness Trainer

http://www.fitnesslink.com
http://www.netsweat.com
From news to links, you'll find it here. You can even ask a fitness trainer a question.

140
Get Fit

http://www.shapeup.org
http://www.justmove.org
Get up, stretch and get moving! These sites promote healthy weight and increased physical activity, with news, exercises and even a fitness diary.

141
Go Girl!

http://www.gogirlmag.com
Get inspired and fit with the help of Melissa Joulwan, editor of, Go girl! Magazine, a sports and fitness magazine for women.

142
Pump It Up

http://www.cyberpump.com
http://www.weightsnet.com
http://www.musclemaster.com
Learn how to build up your physique. Make sure you sign up for Muscle Master's newsletter to get your daily fitness tip via e-mail.

143
Run Like the Wind

http://www.runnersworld.com
http://www.kicksports.com
Check out these cool sites about running and athletic conditioning; beginners, intermediates and advanced are all invited.

144
<u>Yoga and You</u>

http://www.yogaclass.com
http://www.yogasite.com
http://www.yrec.org
Many of us have been exploring yoga, an ancient art whose health benefits have been well documented.

CHAPTER VI
GLORIOUS FOOD

145
Be a Gourmet

http://www.gourmetspot.com
Food, drink, recipes, seasonal ideas and more can be found at this delectable site.

146
Epicurious

http://www.epicurious.com
Looking for anything to do with food and drink? Devour loads of information here.

147
Food TV

http://www.foodtv.com
Everything you ever wanted to know about cooking is here, with a recipe search engine, a marketplace, tips and even how-to videos to help you in the kitchen.

148
Cooking 101

http://www.goodcooking.com
http://www.globalgourmet.com
Cooking 101 starts with these top food and recipe sites, replete with top foods from around the world.

149
Gourmet

http://www.messygourmet.com
http://www.wwrecipes.com
http://www.recipecenter.com
These scrumptious sites include recipes, techniques, equipment and news for the novice or professional chef.

150
Culinary Delight

http://www.kitchenlink.com
With categories of ethnic cooking, health and fitness, everyday cooking, special diets, celebrations and much more, you might spend more time on the Net than in the kitchen.

151
Vegetarians Meet on the Net

http://www.veg.org
http://www.vegweb.com
http://www.vrg.org
These pages are devoted to vegetarian lifestyle, philosophy and recipes.

152
"I'm Tired of Cooking!"

http://www.zagat.com
http://www.trabble.com
Let's dine out tonight. These sites will let you know about restaurants in your area.

153
Diet and Fitness

http://www.ediets.com
http://www.cyberdiet.com
Over two million members enjoy the support and tips at these sites. Need a personal diet profile and some encouragement? Join the community.

154
Diet Right

http://www.dietwatch.com
http://www.dietsite.com
These award-winning diet sites will encourage you in a life long program to look and feel your best.

155
Ask the Dietitian

http://www.dietitian.com
What's your question? This site has some health-conscious answers, from "alcohol" to "zinc."

156
You Are What You Eat

http://www.olen.com/food
http://rover.nhlbi.nih.gov/chd
Learn about the content of the foods you eat — low fat, diet, fast food, cholesterol content and more.

157
Healthy Eating

http://www.tasteforliving.com

"Where food and health meet." This well-designed site offers recipes and nutrition advice and describes how to change your SAD (standard American diet) plate.

158
Nutrition, Nutrition, Nutrition

http://www.nutri-facts.com
http://www.navigator.tufts.edu

These sites have everything you need to know about maintaining a lifestyle of proper nutrition. While you're there, figure out your BMI (body mass index).

159
Arbor Nutrition

http://www.arborcom.com

A must for the educated eater, this site has links to everything from cooking and dining to nutrition, ancient diets, agriculture and the food industry.

160
Nutrition News

http://www.cspinet.org
Learn about the value of food you eat, and read some great articles about nutrition.

161
Cooking Light

http://www.cookinglight.com
The solution to long-term nutrition is cooking good food a little on the light side.

162
Write and Eat

http://www.eatright.org
http://www.writeeating.com
The secret is to eat right and write it down.

163
Calories Do Count

http://www.caloriecontrol.org
Here is everything you need to know about calories and a push to get physical.

164
Heart-Healthy and Heavenly

http://www.deliciousdecisions.org
A heart-healthy, nutritious eating plan doesn't have to be dull. The American Heart Association will show you how.

165
Five a Day

http://www.5aday.gov
Eat five servings a day of fruits and vegetables, and don't forget to exercise. Use the calculator at this site to see how you are performing.

166
The FDA

http://www.foodsafety.gov
Here's your source for food safety information.

CHAPTER VII
HIT THE ROAD

167
Travel with the Best

http://www.johnnyjet.com
http://www.kasbah.com
http://www.tripspot.com
Before you plan your next trip, be sure to visit here for travel directories, maps, guides, brochures and search engines.

168
Book It

http://www.travelocity.com
http://www.expedia.com
http://www.thetrip.com
If you're ready to make travel plans, these sites will help with air, auto and hotel reservations. All of the other travel essentials are also available.

169
The Fairest of the Fares

http://www.lowestfare.com
http://www.bestfares.com
http://www.lowairfare.com
http://www.cheaptickets.com
Why pay more? Get the best possible prices on plane tickets by using these sites.

170
Smart Travel

http://www.smarterliving.com
Be smart; subscribe to the newsletters, read the articles and get travel bargains.

171
Rooms for You

http://www.all-hotels.com
http://www.hotelguide.com
Use these sites to connect to hotels and inns all over the world.

172
What a Deal

http://www.hoteldiscount.com
Are you looking for a deal on a hotel stay? This site guarantees lower rates.

173
Women on the Go

http://www.women-traveling.com
Women Traveling Together's goal is "to bring women together who want to travel and make new friends in a comfortable, small group environment while eliminating the penalties of solo travel."

174
It's Mine!

http://www.mytravelguide.com
It's all yours. Enjoy this travel portal with over a hundred expert guides, articles, message boards and many tools for the frequent traveler.

"Relax mom...it's macaroni."

175
Famous Guides

http://www.fodors.com
http://www.frommers.com
From mini-guides to budget travel, these well-known publications can assist with your next trip.

176
City Guides

http://links.expedia.com/am
http://www.digitalcity.com
From Aachen to Zwolle, you'll learn some interesting items about cities throughout the world.

177
Weather Forecast

http://www.weather.com/travelwise
http://www.worldclimate.com
What's the temperature of Alaska in July, Australia in October or your own zip code right now? These sites will help you stay weatherproof.

178
Car, Train, Plane, Cruise

http://www.bnm.com
http://www.trainweb.com
http://www.airwise.com
http://www.cruising.org

No matter what your desired mode of transportation or type of vacation, they've got you covered.

179
A Walk in the Park

http://www.llbean.com/parksearch
http://parks.yahoo.com
http://www.nps.gov

Park yourself at these sites and discover some of the world's most spectacular scenery, preserved in state and National Parks.

180
World Traveler

http://www.travlang.com
http://www.atlapedia.com
Learn about countries and their customs, and memorize some useful phrases before you go.

181
Travel Healthy

http://www.travelhealth.com
http://www.medicineplanet.com
Review these sites which are dedicated to healthy and safe travel.

182
Legalities

http://www.passportnow.com
http://www.customs.treas.gov
http://www.travel.state.gov
Know the rules concerning passports, customs regulations, the unauthorized destinations and travel warnings.

183
Know Before You Go

http://www.travelsecrets.com
http://www.tips4trips.com
http://www.leisureplanet.com
Find out all about specific destinations with these travel guides. They'll answer your questions, from preplanning to traveling with kids.

184
Family Travel Fun

http://www.familytravelguides.com
http://www.thefamilytravelfiles.com
http://www.familytravelforum.com
Traveling with the kids? These family friendly sites will make it more fun.

185
Pet Companions

http://www.petswelcome.com
http://www.companimalz.com
Let these sites help while traveling with your four-legged companions.

186
<u>A World of Vacation Ideas</u>

http://www.learningvacations.com
Golf, cooking, adventure and more are available as you travel and learn.

187
<u>Shop Around for Vacations</u>

http://www.spectrav.com
http://www.vacationspot.com
Research, plan, price and purchase your dream vacation. If it's not here, it probably doesn't exist.

188
<u>TV Travels</u>

http://www.savvytraveler.org
http://www.travelchannel.com
These television travel channels have online companions. Learn about all the great places to visit, and at least take a virtual tour.

189
Listen Up!

http://www.travelersjournal.com
http://www.travelupdate.com
Daily, listen to news about interesting travel destinations.

190
Travel Wear and Gear

http://www.rei.com
http://www.travelsmith.com
http://www.randmcnallystore.com
These stores will suit your needs for everything concerning travel.

191
Food for Thought

http://www.zagat.com
http://www.vicinity.com/mcdonalds
At these sites, you'll locate fine dining, casual eateries and even where to find the next McDonald's.

192
A View From…

http://www.earthcam.com
http://www.cammunity.com
…cameras all over the world.

193
You Deserve a Break

http://www.spafinders.com
Have you been to a spa lately? Search for one online.

CHAPTER VIII
IN THE KNOW

194
Want to Learn?

http://www.soyouwanna.com
They'll "teach you how to do all the things nobody taught you in school" here.

195
Wired for Information

http://www.backwire.com
Backwire offers, for free, over thirty newsletters covering many different topics.

196
Zooba?

http://www.zooba.com
Receive easy-to-read e-mail about more than forty subject areas. From "biography" to "travel," you'll enjoy these simple but informative Zooba mailings.

197
Search Engines

http://www.yahoo.com
http://www.altavista.com
http://www.excite.com
http://www.lycos.com
Here are a few of the major search engines. Be careful of information overload; there's billions of Web sites out there.

198
MetaSearch

http://www.northernlight.com
http://www.dogpile.com
http://www.profusion.com
Search engines have spawned "meta search engines." These will search multiple engines simultaneously, giving you a multitude of information on your chosen topic.

199
Simple Rules

http://www.google.com
http://www.simpli.com
http://www.invisibleweb.com
Try these simple but elegant search engines.

200
Information, Please

http://www.phonenumbers.net
http://www.theultimates.com
Look for anyone's e-mail address or phone number by using these search engines.

201
Jeeves, Answer This

http://www.askjeeves.com
No problem! Ask Jeeves almost any question, and he'll come up with Web sites that
will provide the answer.

202
G-Rated Search

http://www.ajkids.com

http://www.familyfriendlysearch.com

http://www.alfy.com

Need a search engine or a portal you're comfortable letting the kids use? These sites meet the challenge.

203
S.O.S

http://www.pcsupport.com

http://www.myhelpdesk.com

Flummoxed by a computer or software issue? These folks will be happy to help. There's even online, real-time support available.

204
Ask an Expert

http://www.askme.com
http://www.allexperts.com
http://www.expertcentral.com

These experts are ready, willing and able to answer your questions. Just pick your category, and find the proper expert for your question.

205
E-Commerce Disclosed

http://www.gomez.com

Gomez rates online commerce sites. Travel, finance, shopping, home and garden and many more are available.

206
Reference This

http://www.refdesk.com

Bob Drudge spends a lot of time on the Net categorizing all the best reference sites.

207
Reference Books on the Web

http://www.ipl.org/ref
http://www.infoplease.com
These sites turn your computer into the starting point for the world's biggest information source.

208
School Reporting

http://www.theschoolreport.com
This site provides information and test results to identify school districts that meet your family's educational needs and goals.

209
Homework Helpers

http://www.bigchalk.com
http://www.studyweb.com
Don't know the answer? Let these interesting sites help the kids log on and learn.

"No, it's not the baby's web page."

210
Words, Words, Words

http://www.m-w.com
http://www.thesaurus.com
http://www.yourdictionary.com

These are dream spots for word lovers, super scholars and atrocious spellers. The Merriam-Webster site even allows you to place a dictionary on your browser.

211
Encyclopedia

http://www.britannica.com
http://encarta.msn.com
http://www.encyclopedia.com

No more expensive, hard-bound, multi-volume books. These encyclopedias have everything their predecessors had and much more.

212
A Word to the Wise

http://www.wordsmith.org
http://www.grammarnow.com
http://www.work-detective.com
These word sites will help build and enhance your vocabulary and grammar.

213
Newspapers

http://www.thepaperboy.com
This paperboy delivers newspapers from all over the world. Cuddle up to the screen, and read your favorite daily journal.

214
Headline News

http://www.1stheadlines.com
http://www.frontpagedailynews.com
http://www.headlinenews.com
Get a quick dose of news at these sites.

215
Network News

http://www.cnn.com
http://abcnews.go.com
http://cbsnews.cbs.com
http://www.msnbc.com
The major networks have complete and timely news on the Net.

216
Weekly News

http://www.newsweek.com
http://www.time.com
http://www.usnews.com
It's time for your weekly news from Newsweek, Time and U.S. News and World Report.

217
O, Say Can You See?

http://www.thisnation.com
http://www.politics.com
http://www.allpolitics.com
http://www.aboutpolitics.com
Are you a political junkie? These sites will keep you plugged in to the process.

218
Be a Maven

http://www.maven.businessweek.com
Business Week knows computers and technology, offering its computer buying guide
and articles from its "Technology & You" column.

219
High-Tech Sites

http://www.techsightings.com
Get daily reviews of the best high-tech sites on the Net.

220
<u>Science Today</u>

http://www.sciencedaily.com
http://www.scienceagogo.com
As quickly as the world of science advances, the Web is the only way to keep up with changes and news. It's educational, interesting and fun.

CHAPTER IX
SAFE AT HOME

221
Only the Best

http://www.bestplaces.net
Over 1,000 cities are evaluated in categories that include housing, costs of living, crime, education, economy, health and climate. See where your hometown fits in.

222
Home and Garden

http://www.hgtv.com
http://www.bhglive.com
Here's an example of a great TV show and magazine making a smooth transition to the Net. You'll find links that lead you to projects, trends, food sites and more.

223
Real People, Real Projects

http://www.hometime.com
http://www.bobvila.com
Derived from the popular TV home improvement shows, these sites offer help on all sorts of home improvement projects, with plenty of how-to-do-it tips.

224
Ask the Builder

http://www.askbuild.com
Tim Carter, a syndicated columnist, has been offering advice and articles on the Net for some time. You can even ask him a question.

225
Do It Yourself

http://www.diyonline.com
http://www.doityourself.com
For those people who love doing their own projects, these sites will help with home improvements, repairs, gardening and more.

226
Fix It Now

http://www.repairclinic.com
http://www.repairnow.com
http://www.naturalhandyman.com
If it's not broken, don't fix it. If it is broken, check here for tips, parts and service solutions for appliances and more throughout your home.

227
Find a Professional

http://www.improvenet.com
Looking for a contractor? This site has pioneered finding contractors via the Net.

228
Home Improvements

http://www.livinghome.com
http://www.housenet.com
Make the most of your environment with home improvements and some design suggestions for every kind of project.

229
Household Problem Solutions
http://www.haleyshints.com/freehints_frame.html
Visit this site for household hints to many common problems and issues.

230
Hints from Heloise
http://www.heloise.com
Since 1959, Heloise and her mom have been providing hints to keep our homes in great shape. Check out her top ten.

231
Mr. Clean
http://www.mrclean.com
On the Net, Mr. Clean answers questions and will help with quick cleanup solutions.

232
Stain Removal
http://www.chemistry.co.nz/stain.htm
From acids to wood sap, this guide will make removing stains a snap.

233
Use It

http://www.wackyuses.com

Learn how to use everyday products in unusual, helpful ways. To clean a toilet, for example, drop in two Alka-Seltzer tablets, wait twenty minutes, brush and flush.

234
The Organized Woman

http://www.organizedhome.com
http://www.getorganizednow.com

Here are practical strategies to simplify your life and environment.

235
Work at Home

http://www.homeofficelife.com

Here are loads of tips to help organize your home office and to make your life just a little bit easier.

236
Home Magazines
http://www.megahomemags.com
Review this list of hundreds of home-oriented magazines for purchase.

237
Incredible Decorating Ideas
http://www.decoratorsecrets.com
http://www.goodhome.com
http://www.homeportfolio.com
These sites offer great advice, tips and items to help make your house into your dream home.

238
Furniture Online
http://www.furniture.com
http://www.furniturefind.com
Purchasing furniture online has come of age. Take these sites for a spin, and spruce up a room or two.

"My family changed the password and locked
me out of the computer. They caught me
downloading tofu recipes."

239
Shed Some Light…

http://www.lampstore.com

…on the subject. Look at hundreds of lamps for every room and environment.

240
Garden ORG or COM

http://www.garden.org

http://www.garden.com

Whether you go to the organization (.org) or to the commercial (.com) Web site, you will be treated to magnificent pictures and helpful tips to make your garden grow.

241
Garden Community

http://www.vg.com

http://www.gardenweb.com

http://www.gardenguides.com

These guides will assist with tips, timely information and ideas for making your garden captivating.

242
<u>Ask Earl</u>

http://www.yardcare.com
Got a question about your yard? Earl is here to give you an answer.

CHAPTER X
SHOPPING BLOCK

243
Safe Shopping

http://www.safeshopping.org
http://www.truste.org
Follow the guidelines set out in these sites to make your online shopping safer.

244
It's Rated

http://www.bizrate.com
Very few sites on the Net rate the online sellers, but this site is one of them. You'll see the Bizrate logo on many Web sites.

245
Easy as 1-2-3

http://www.shoponline123.com
The editors of this credible publication offer tips on how to buy online, as well as reviews of hundreds of shopping sites.

246
Coupons and Rebates

http://www.hotcoupons.com
http://www.coolsavings.com
http://www.cyberrebate.com
There's no reason to pay full price for anything. Get coupons and rebate offers at these sites.

247
Half Bay

http://www.ebay.com
http://www.half.com
You can go to the famous E-bay site to bid on items or to another company it owns to buy used items at half price.

248
Mall Mania

http://www.mega-mall.net
http://www.storesatoz.com
http://www.reallybigmall.com

These huge shopping sites will link you directly to stores. They're divided by category to save you time.

249
The Sale Times

http://www.salescircular.com

What's on sale at retail stores this week? This site has the answer.

250
Product Review

http://www.productopia.com

These independent reviewers offer advice on more than 625 product categories.

251
Comparison Shopping

http://www.mysimon.com
http://www.dealtime.com
http://www.bottomdollar.com
http://www.pricescan.com
When you're searching for the best combination of value, price and style, check these sites. They'll link you with the best buys on the Web.

252
Catalog Shopper

http://www.cataloglink.com
http://www.skymall.com
http://catalog.savvy.com
Love those catalogs? You can find them online or even order them here via snail mail.

253
<u>A Passion for Fashion</u>

http://www.fashionmall.com
http://www.shoppingtheworld.com
http://www.designeroutlet.com
From fancy footwear to designer clothing, these fashion sources will keep you dressed to the nines.

254
<u>Fun and Funky</u>

http://www.girlshop.com
http://www.purpleskirt.com
Funky and fabulous, these sites will help you make your own fashion statement.

255
<u>Shopping Bug</u>

http://www.bluefly.com
Here are some designers and great deals. Best of all, you can create your own personalized catalog.

256
New Mom

http://www.estyle.com
http://www.babyshoe.com
Be in style with selections for maternity, baby and kids. While you're there, ask Cindy Crawford a question, and read what she recommends.

257
Sporting a Great Look

http://www.athleta.com
http://www.electrasports.com
From the slopes to the ropes, you'll be in style no matter which sport you gravitate to. Just going to these sites will make you feel fit.

258
Smart Starts

http://www.zanybrainy.com
http://www.smarterkids.com
Shop at these top-of-the-line stores for educational toys, software and some stimulating stuff to keep your kids challenged and thinking.

259
<u>Toy Manufacturers of America</u>

http://www.toy-tma.org

What toys are the best sellers? This industry trade organization has the answer to that question and many others.

260
<u>Toy Time</u>

http://www.toysrus.com

http://www.fao.com

http://www.etoys.com

From "brick-and-mortar" stores to "click and order," now you can enjoy the great selection of products with the convenience of ordering from home.

261
<u>Cool Teen Stuff</u>

http://www.karmakiss.com

http://www.2grrrls.com

She knows what she likes — today. These trendy sites will help her see what's new and what's not.

262
Antiques and Collectibles

http://www.tias.com
This portal to antiques and collectibles has over 1,300 categories and 260,000 items for you to peruse.

263
It's a Good Thing

http://www.marthabymail.com
http://www.cooking.com
Here are pretty and practical accessories to beautify your home and make work a little easier, especially in the kitchen.

264
Hooked on Shopping

http://www.hsn.com
http://www.qvc.com
Have we got a deal for you! These well-known TV shopping clubs are online and ready and willing to sell to you, 24/7.

265
Online Gift Giving

http://www.ugive.com

There are over 5,000 items from which to choose. Select a few of them, and the choices are delivered to the recipient immediately via email. That person then gets to pick his or her own present. It's a unique way to give a gift.

266
Gift Certificates

http://www.giftcertificates.com
http://www.surprise.com

Not sure of what to buy? Give a gift certificate, or get suggestions at Surprise.

267
Only the Best

http://www.luxuryfinder.com

If you live in the lap of luxury, stop by this site. It's got a magazine and many fine items for the discriminating buyer.

"I've grossed over two million dollars since
I started advertising my business on the Internet!"

268
Shop for a Cause

http://www.shop2give.com
http://www.greatergood.com
http://www.npsmall.com
Shop at these sites, and portions of proceeds will be donated to worthy causes.

269
Going, Going, Gone!

http://www.priceline.com
http://www.auctioninsider.com
http://www.auctionrover.com
http://www.auctionwatch.com
On the Net, you can bid for almost anything, and many people have made a hobby or business out of placing their items up for auction.

270
As Seen on TV

http://www.asotv.com
Here's a smorgasbord of special things you can buy online, from books to greeting cards to things you've seen on infomercials on TV.

271
Incredible Edibles

http://www.chocoholic.com
http://www.chocolatevault.com
http://www.igourmet.com
http://www.giftcorp.com
If you've got the appetite, we've got the Web site, for everything from chocolates to life's other little luxurious indulgences.

272
The Good Old Days

http://www.hometownfavorites.com
Do you talk about the products you consumed back in the 1950s? Forget memory lane; now you can purchase those products.

273
What a Bargain

http://www.bargaindog.com
http://www.freebitz.com
http://www.thefreesite.com
Just click these sites to learn about bargains and tons of free stuff.

CHAPTER XI
FUN, FUN, FUN

274
<u>We're Having a Party!</u>

http://www.birthdayexpress.com

http://www.birthdayinabox.com

So you want to have a party? These sites are crammed with tips, decorating ideas, recipes and even how to draw up the perfect guest list.

275
<u>You're Invited</u>

http://www.evite.com

http://www.eparties.com

http://www.seeuthere.com

Ask a friend to lunch, or plan a party. Online invitations are easy with these fun, free invitation services.

276
The Hostess with the Mostest

http://entertaining.about.com

http://www.visatablelinen.com

Make your party picture-perfect with practical tips, including how to set a table for any occasion.

277
Parties and Gatherings

http://www.greatentertaining.com

Here's a one-stop shopping location for life's celebrations. There's even a section for "girl gatherings."

278
I'll Drink to That

http://www.webtender.com

http://www.idrink.com

Having a party? Let's make a toast. Here's to knowing how to mix any kind of drink.

279
Holiday Fun

http://www.holidays.net
Everyone loves holidays. Enjoy and plan for them using the Internet.

280
Awesome Greeting Cards

http://www.bluemountain.com
http://www.greeting-cards.com
Send a greeting for any occasion—perhaps a singing birthday-gram or a musical anniversary wish. Save a tree, and it's free!

281
Scrapbooking

http://www.scrapnetwork.com
http://www.creativescrapbooking.com
Become a part of the national craze for creating fun, memorable and informative scrapbooks. Read articles, and find out what the pros are doing.

282
Say Cheese

http://www.wolfcamera.com
http://www.kodak.com
http://www.zing.com

Capture the world with your camera. Here are sites that will allow you to take advantage of your hobby in the digital world.

283
Hobby Happy

http://www.ehobbies.com
http://www.hobbysearch.com

Whatever you're interested in, from growing orchids to stitching quilts to building model airplanes with your kids, you'll find detailed information and supply sources on the Web.

284
Family Fun

http://www.familyfun.com
http://www.thefamilycorner.com
http://www.totcity.com
http://www.discoverykids.com
What could be better than family fun? Here are some wholesome activities and entertainment for the entire family.

285
Genealogy 101

http://www.cyndislist.com
http://www.familyhistory.com
http://www.familytreemaker.com
Consult these resources to learn about and trace your family history.

286
Book Lover

http://www.bookspot.com
How many books do you read? Curl up to this site and read all about books, writers and resources.

287
Museums Galore

http://www.museumnetwork.com
From arts to zoos, you'll find 'em all here—over 30,000 of them. Just think, no lines or screaming kids.

288
All Eyes on Art

http://www.artcyclopedia.com
This online fine art search engine features over 7,500 great artists.

289
The Sporting Life

http://www.sportsline.com
http://www.foxsports.com
http://www.espn.com
http://www.cnnsi.com
Here is everything you ever wanted to know about the world of sports.

290
<u>TV for Kids</u>

http://www.ctw.org
http://www.cartoonnetwork.com
http://www.nick.com
http://www.pbs.org/kids
These great TV stations have Web sites, too.

291
<u>Your Real Audio Guide</u>

http://www.realguide.com
One of the most exciting technologies on the Internet is RealAudio. This site will guide you to many of the fine audio and video sites.

292
<u>Let's Go See…</u>

http://www.tourdates.com
http://www.pollstar.com
http://www.ticketmaster.com
…a concert. Use these sites to find any concert anywhere. Then go ahead and buy the tickets online.

293
It's Movie Time

http://www.imdb.com

http://www.moviefone.com

You'll find every movie ever filmed, reviews and where and when they are playing.

294
You Can't See That!

http://www.screenit.com

Want to know what movies are appropriate for your kids? This site gives you the inside scoop.

295
Did You Say Gossip?

http://www.gossipcentral.com

http://www.gossip.com

Get the latest on all your favorite celebrities.

296
Game Time

http://www.okbridge.com
http://www.uproar.com
http://www.jigzone.com
The Internet is a great source of free games, quizzes, jigsaw puzzles and trivia. Try your hand at these fun sites.

297
Trivia

http://www.uselessknowledge.com
http://www.funtrivia.com
http://www.primate.wisc.edu/people/hamel/trivia.html
Trivia can be a lot of fun, and the Net offers a lot of it.

298
A Puzzle A Day Keeps the Cobwebs Away

http://www.dailypuzzler.com
http://www.thinks.com
These sites are where to go for your daily fix of crossword puzzles, word games, logic games, jumbles, word searches and trivia.

299
It's a Classic

http://hoyle.won.net
http://www.station.sony.com
Classic games such as Hearts, Spades, Bridge, Jeopardy, Wheel of Fortune and many more are available at these sites.

300
Internet Addiction?

http://www.netaddiction.com
The Internet is a great place to hang out. However, if you find yourself neglecting too many offline things, you might want to spend a little bit of time at this site.

INDEX (BY SITE NUMBER)

INDEX (BY SITE NUMBER)

Index (by Site Number)

The Incredible Newsletter

If you are enjoying this book, you can also arrange to receive a steady stream of more "incredible Internet things," delivered directly to your e-mail address.

The Leebow Letter, Ken Leebow's weekly e-mail newsletter, provides new sites, updates on existing ones and information about other happenings on the Internet.

For more details about *The Leebow Letter* and how to subscribe, visit us at:

WWW.300INCREDIBLE.COM

(USO) United Service Organizations

For nearly 60 years, the United Service Organizations (USO) has "Delivered America" to service members stationed around the world, thousands of miles from family and friends. The USO provides celebrity entertainment, recreation, cultural orientation, language training, travel assistance, telephone and Internet access, and other vital services to military personnel and their families at 115 locations worldwide. The USO is a non-profit organization, not a government agency. It relies on the generosity of corporations and individuals to enable its programs and services to continue. For more information on contributing to the USO, please call 1-800-876-7469 or visit its Web site at www.uso.org.